Wisdom without waffle

Dear Frances,

Thanks again!

lots of love,

Sandy

Wisdom without waffle

BY SANDY C. NEWBIGGING

New Beginnings
PUBLISHING

About the author

Sandy Newbigging gained an honours degree in international management and worked as a management development consultant before going on to train in life coaching, neuro-linguistic programming and other forms of therapy.

By just 25 years old, Sandy had already become a successful life coach, author and trainer. He is the founder of 'Momentum Coaching & Training' and 'Confident Kids & Teens'. He is also the author of another book called 'New Beginnings' and a 5CD audio programme called 'You Can Do It'.

For more info visit www.sandynewbigging.com.

Acknowledgements

I would like to thank my parents, John and Sandra, and my brother Max, for their unconditional love, support and encouragement.

I am very appreciative to Susan Burnell for allowing me to use one of her fantastic images for the front cover of the book.

I am also grateful to Jonathan and Lyndsey Brigain, Gemma Smith and Bryce Redford for providing me with valuable feedback relating to the design and content of the book.

Finally, I would like to thank all of my coaching clients and workshop attendees. You have all taught and inspired me so much.

I wrote this book because...

Simplicity is paramount to enjoying a stress-free life. Simple is sustainable. Simple is easy and simple is flexible. On the other hand, complicated is often busy and stressful. Complicated takes time to manage and usually distracts people from what's really important. This book aims to provide timeless wisdom in a simple, straightforward and practical way.

His Holiness the Dalai Lama once said, *"Sometimes not getting what you think you want is a wonderful stroke of luck"*. I love this quote. It has helped me remain optimistic during challenging times and taught me that less words really do say more.

Sandy C. Newbigging, July 2005

How to use this book...

This book is full of insights that have the power to transform your life forever. You can read the book in the usual way from cover to cover. Or you can hold a question or problem in your mind and open the book at the page(s) that feel right to you. Either way, you will find yourself drawn to the wisdom that is most relevant and perfect for you, each time you choose to pick up the book.

The insights can be interpreted in many ways, so I encourage you to look for the meaning beyond the words, the hidden insights that may not be obvious at first glance. Enjoy the book!

Wisdom without waffle

If you want to see different
results in your life, then start
by looking at things
differently.

Be courageous. Go beyond casual
chitchat.

It's ok to say, "I don't know".

Complaining corrodes your power.
Do something.

Decide what you want.

You always have a choice
- so choose!

Be nice to yourself.

Getting stressed is pointless.

You get what you focus on.
So focus on what you want.

Holding grudges hurts the hands that hold them.

Love heals hurts.

Let go of the past because it has let go of you.

Resist the temptation to gossip.

Things always happen at the perfect time in the perfect way.

Accept that things are perfect.
Especially the things you think
aren't.

Believe.

Love things perfectly instead of trying to find perfect things to love.

Ask for what you want.

It's ok if you don't always get what you ask for.

Everyone is always doing their best - including you!

Stop selling. Start attracting.

Focus on what is real.
Be here now.

Know the destination.
Enjoy the journey.

Stop needing stuff.
Travel light.

Let go.

Put yourself first. It's the only way you can truly help others.

Give what you want away without
expecting anything back.

Only talk if it improves upon
the silence.

Shine.

There is great strength in
vulnerability.

The more you share about yourself, the more other people have to love about you.

Be yourself.

Everyone's unique so there's no point comparing.

Take 100% responsibility for
your life.

Whatever you do, have fun!

Take the initiative.

You do know - even when you think you don't.

Recycle.

Be interested as well as interesting.

Separation is an illusion.

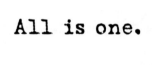

Be compassionate.

Love yourself.

Say "YES" as much as possible.

Act now.

Always look for the best in yourself and others.

Listen beyond words.
Look beyond looks.

Learn from the past without it dictating the future.

Be willing to receive the best.

Do yourself a favour by doing
someone else one.

Help others to help themselves.

Avoid trying to impress.

Be self-motivated.

Enjoy all weather.

Notice, appreciate and enjoy the little things in life.

Let each moment be a new beginning.

You have a voice. Use it wisely.

Be playful.

Aim to find agreement.

Look after your body.

Breathe deeply.

Life is now.

Look up more often.

Whether something is possible or not is merely a matter of opinion.

You ARE good enough.

Play to your strengths.

You are stronger than you think.

Remember to wake up each day.

If you want to see something inspirational, then look in a mirror!

You are what you think you are
and you become what you think
you will become.

You are the thinker of your thoughts. If they aren't useful, change them.

You're a human being, not a human doing. Just be more often.

Never try to meditate.
That defeats its purpose.

You always have more than you think you do.

You are always more than you
think you are.

Embrace challenges.
They help you grow and keep life
interesting.

The most difficult decisions
usually have the greatest
rewards.

Respect other people's beliefs.

Treat everyone equally.

Observe without judgement.

Connect rather than compete.

You can be alone without feeling
lonely.

Enjoy your own company.

Listen.

Notice the moon.

Share.

Smile.

Take things less seriously.

Take nothing personally.

Make eye contact.

Remember people's names.

Slow down.

Text less. Talk more.

NEVER drop litter.

Be on time.

Encourage yourself and others.

Trust your instincts.

Go the extra mile.

Respect our world.

When you change, everything changes.

Decide how you want to be and be it now.

Change is instant.

Surprise yourself.

Walk places.

Never underestimate the impact
of a kind smile.

Accept compliments.

Feel your feelings.

Dance.

Celebrate every day.

If you want to love your time
on earth then choose to love
your time on earth.
It's that simple!

Don't wait.

Go for it!

You are more confident than you
think.

The secret of long-term life
fulfilment is to enjoy less,
more.

To love without reasons is to fully embrace the moment you're in.

Commitment transforms
possibility into inevitability.

It's ok that things are taking
as long as they are taking.

Get out of your thoughts; get
into the moment and notice.

You arrived the day you were born. There is nowhere to get to. You are perfect, whole and complete as you are now.

Make gratefulness your way of life.

Say, "I love you" as often as you think it.

Simplify.

Less words, say more.

Also by Sandy C. Newbigging...

New Beginnings

What if you could attract your goals with effortless ease and live even more joyfully?

Every moment of every day is a new beginning. A new opportunity to create the life you want. In this life-changing book, Sandy Newbigging reveals how you can make every day a celebration. He shares insightful ways to embrace the new, let go of problems, attract what you want and live joyfully.

ISBN: 0-9550770-0-1

For information on talks or workshops
given by Sandy Newbigging or to book him
for a speaking event please email:

info@sandynewbigging.com

Or visit:

www.sandynewbigging.com